This book belongs to

....

stick your photo here

About Katha

Katha, a nonprofit organization founded in 1988, works in the literacy to literature continuum. We work with slum communities and municipal corporation schools to ensure that every child learns to read for fun and at grade level. We also work with women and teachers so that all children achieve their potential.

Our books, workshops and learning centres strive to forge cross-cultural connections through story and Story Pedagogy©. As one of India's finest publishers, our initiative has been recognized as "a unique and special moment in Indian publishing history," by *The Economic Times*.

Katha's books have received global recognition, including the nomination by an international jury for the prestigious Astrid Lindgren Award, the world's largest prize for children's literature.

We love to work with new and established writers, translators and illustrators.

Do you like writing, illustrating, translating for children? Write to us at editors@katha.org to become a cherished member of the Katha family!

"An educational jewel in India's crown." — **Naoyuki Shinohara, Deputy Managing Director, International Monetary Fund**

"Katha stands as an exemplar for all the creative projects around the world that grapple with ordinary and dramatic misery in cities."
— **Charles Landry, The Art of City Making**

"Katha has a real soft corner for kids. Which is why it … create[s] such gorgeous picture books for children." — **Time Out**

Katha's work is driven by the idea that children can bring change to their communities that is sustainable and real, just as the children do in [their books.] — **Papertigers**

Razia
and her Pink Elephant

Mukul Dube
Art by Fahad Faizal

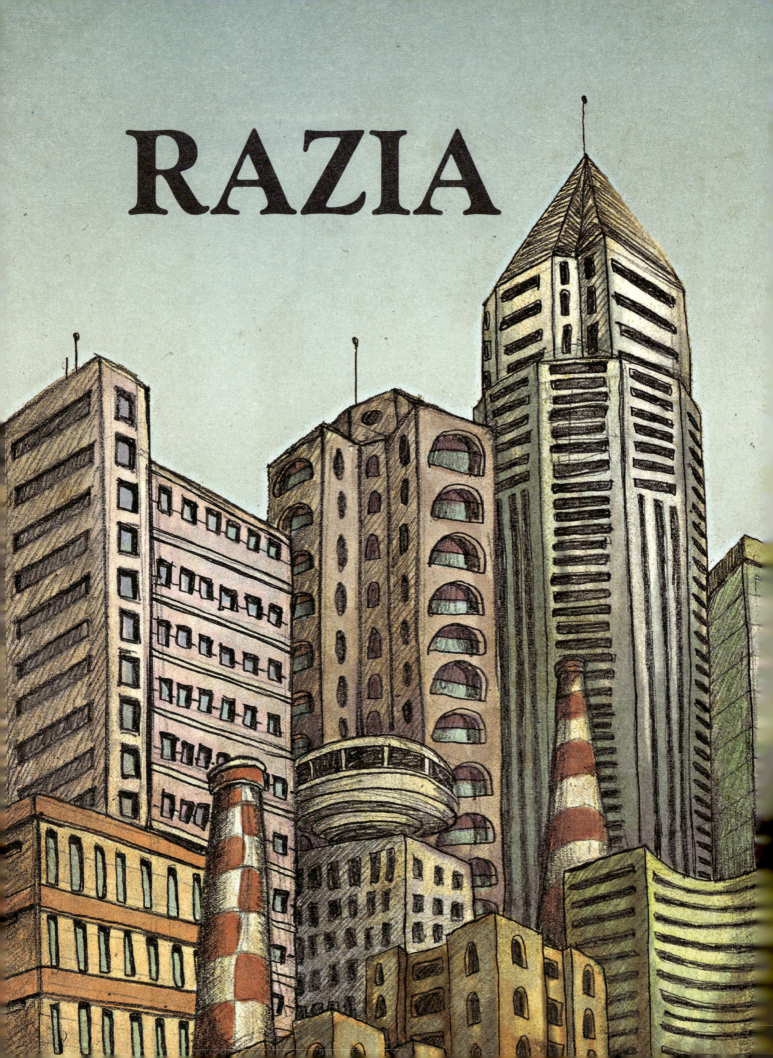

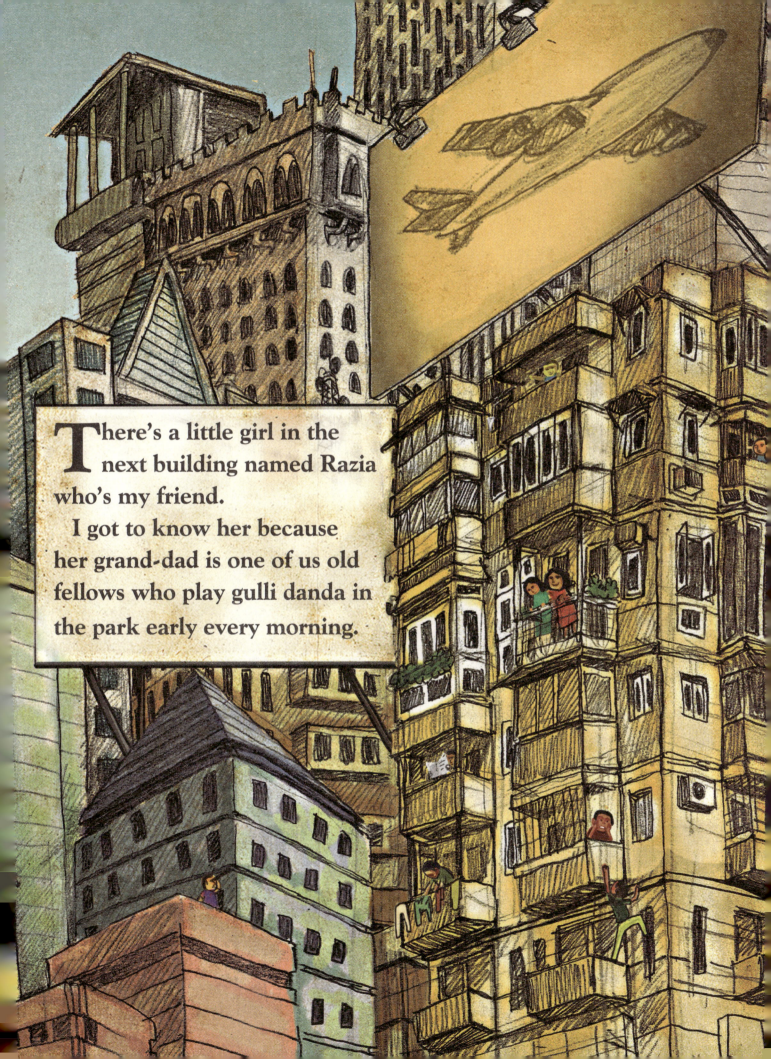

There's a little girl in the next building named Razia who's my friend.

I got to know her because her grand-dad is one of us old fellows who play gulli danda in the park early every morning.

Some other old fellows run around the park and some walk fast and huff and puff and swing their arms – but my gang, we play gulli danda. Maybe we will play in the Olympics one day, or at least in the Patna Asian Games.

Razia's grand-dad doesn't always hit the gulli with the danda, specially when he forgets to put on his glasses, but he is the best catcher in the team. No flying gulli can ever pass him. He jumps high, he leaps to this side or that, and he snatches it out of the air. In one hand he holds his walking stick. But – oops. I shouldn't be talking about him: after all, this story is about Razia.

Razia's dad Ramesh works in a big, shiny office building which has blue desks, red chairs, and wall-to-wall computers in every room. The boss is a bad lady who doesn't let anyone play games on the computers. They are only allowed to do dull, dull work all day long.

It is true that they do important work – they keep the trains running on time and they make sure that the chickens lay enough eggs and all kinds of other things – but Razia's dad thinks that they would be happier if they could play Pong every now and then. He says that happy people work better than sad people.

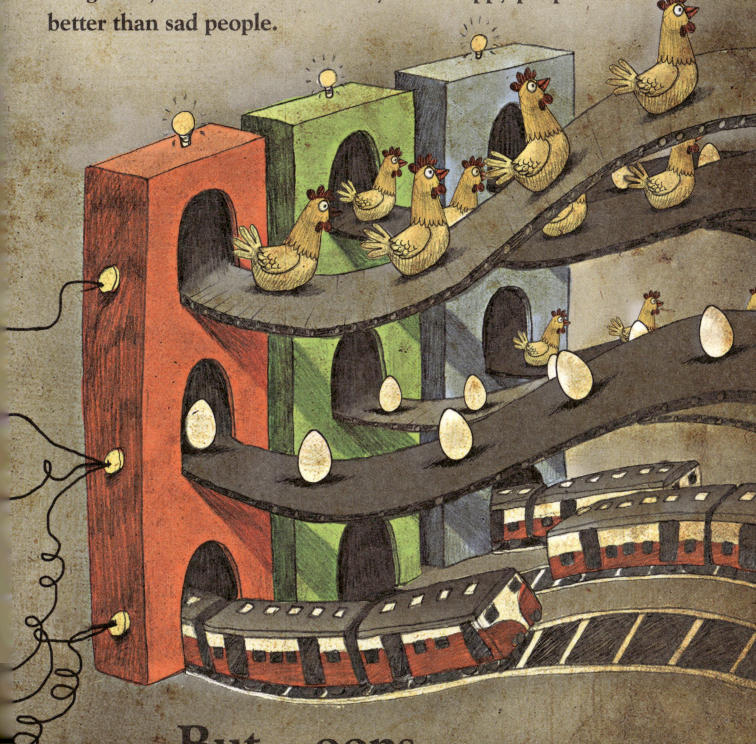

But – oops. This story is about Razia.

Sarasvati is a pink elephant who was born near the river Periyar in Kerala. She was born pink. I have to say this because some silly people like to argue that she was grey or green or blue, any odd colour that comes into their heads, before Razia painted her pink. They don't understand that my Razia is a busy girl who has no time to go about painting baby elephants.

Sarasvati's mummy, Mariamma Kutty, was very big and used to work at the temple in Kozhikode. Actually she didn't have that much work to do. People would put different colours on her forehead and her trunk and her big, flappy ears. They would drape fine cloths of silk and velvet over her and they would hang golden chains around her neck.

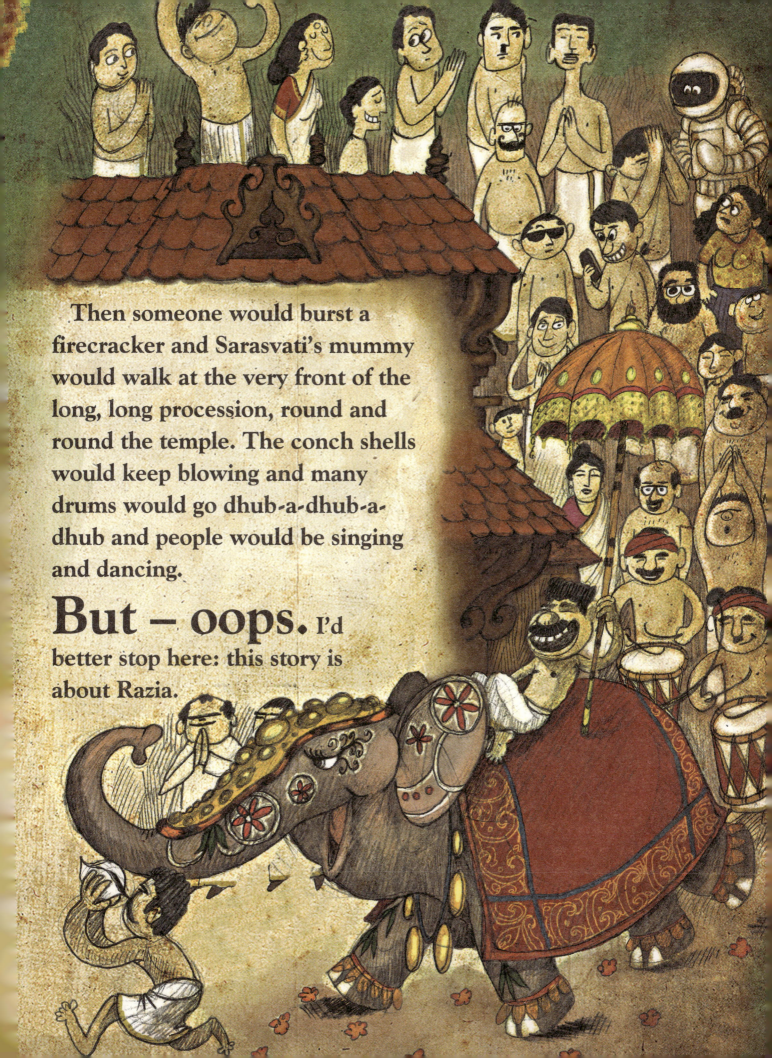

Then someone would burst a firecracker and Sarasvati's mummy would walk at the very front of the long, long procession, round and round the temple. The conch shells would keep blowing and many drums would go dhub-a-dhub-a-dhub and people would be singing and dancing.

But – oops. I'd better stop here: this story is about Razia.

Mariamma Kutty's youngest brother Sher Singh was a funny fellow. He was a very strong elephant, and also very headstrong. He liked travelling and going to new places. So he would never stay in one job for more than five years. Elephants have very long lives, as everyone knows, so five years is only a short time to them. As soon as five years were up, he would hand in his papers, and off he would go.

He had been to Australia, and everyone was amazed that he could hop higher than the kangaroos and at the same time shear seven sheep in a minute.

For five years he worked in the Perth Zoo, looking after a family of Tasmanian Devils.

Sher Singh was Sarasvati's mama, and he was a very loving mama. From Australia he brought her a toy boomerang which she used to practise throwing with her trunk. When it came back, she would catch it too with her trunk.

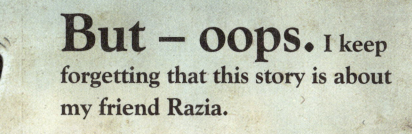

But – oops. I keep forgetting that this story is about my friend Razia.

Next time I'll be more careful. But for now – bye-bye and ta-ta. I have to take my pet goose for her evening walk. If I don't do that, I won't get an egg for my breakfast.

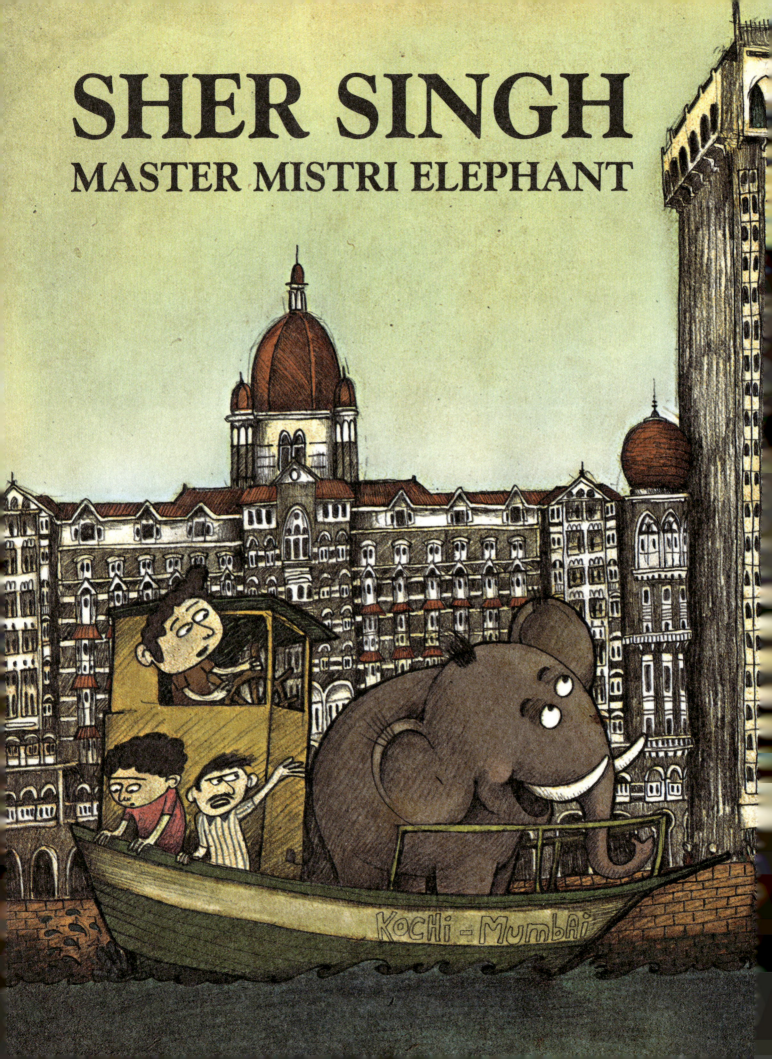

Well, let me tell you a bit more about Sher Singh and how he became a brilliant mechanic. It happened like this. After school he went to Mumbai to work in a carrot canning factory as Chief Taster.

A Carrot Taster is like a Tea Taster, who only tastes the tea but does not drink it. Wine Tasters do the same, and Chocolate Tasters too. I feel very sorry for Chocolate Tasters. So Sher Singh would only crrrrunch! on a carrot but would not swallow it. After each tasting he would rinse out his mouth with coconut water (he was born in Kerala, you see, and Malayalis are coconut freaks) so that his taste buds would be clean and fresh for the next tasting.

Sher Singh was such a good carrot taster that the factory became very successful and its tins went everywhere. Even the Queen of Holland and the Emperor of Japan used to munch carrots which Sher Singh had passed as fit for royal consumption. The "Penguin Journal", a magazine published in Antarctica, once had a photo of Sher Singh on its cover. In the story inside he was called Tiger Lion the Carrot King. The birds had translated his name too! Maybe it was too cold there for their brains to work properly.

Meanwhile, because he was such a genius, the factory had also begun canning pumpkins, prawns, jalebis and even fried goose eggs.

Oops ... the story.

Sorry. I get distracted easily. I was telling you how Sher Singh became an expert mechanic. In the evenings, after he had tasted many sacks full of carrots, he used to stroll down to the Gateway of India to feed the pigeons. Why did he go there always, when there were pigeons all over the city of Mumbai? Aha! Yes, you guessed it. He was a Malayali elephant, so he loved coconuts, and right next to the Gateway of India there were many, many people selling fresh coconuts. So he would gulp and gobble a few dozen coconuts and then feed the pigeons. There was one, Natasha, who became his special friend. But I shall tell you about her some other time. Let me stick to the story.

After feeding the pigeons, Sher Singh would hop on to the local train and go to the United India Tuskers' Club in Bandra.

Most of Mumbai's elephants used to gather there, and also visiting foreign elephants.

One evening at the Club, Sher Singh met U Kant, a philosophical German elephant who had spent many years in Myanmar and become a full Burmese citizen – he even had an Official Myanmar Elephant Passport. U Kant was a great engineer, perhaps even the best ever.

He was very old, and even Albert Einstein had ridden on his back. He had learnt his trade in the saw-mills and on the river barges and the ocean steamers.

He had been called to Mumbai to advise the Trombay people on their brand new atomic reactor, which was so big that only an elephant could work it.

Well, old U Kant liked Sher Singh very much. They soon became firm friends and he taught the young fellow all he knew about all kinds of machines. That was how Sher Singh became a Master Mistri.

There's also a wonderful story about the many-wheeled cycle that Sher Singh built for himself when he was in Sydney. But I'll tell you that one next time. If I write too much now the Editor may be angry and may speak to my pet goose – and then I won't get a breakfast egg. We should all live in fear of editors and geese.

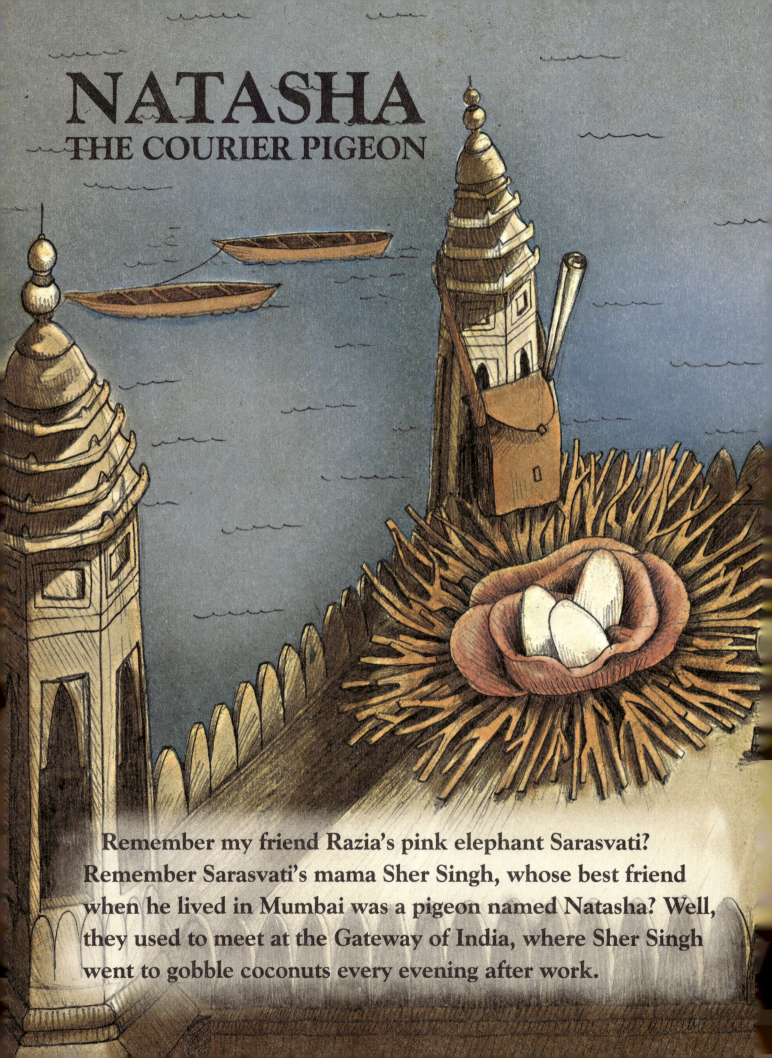

NATASHA
THE COURIER PIGEON

Remember my friend Razia's pink elephant Sarasvati? Remember Sarasvati's mama Sher Singh, whose best friend when he lived in Mumbai was a pigeon named Natasha? Well, they used to meet at the Gateway of India, where Sher Singh went to gobble coconuts every evening after work.

Natasha's Residence-cum-Office-Nest was right on top of the Gateway. She had been given this privilege by the Mayor of Mumbai.

Other birds had to build their nests at bus stations and cinema houses and fish markets and skating rinks and ice cream parlours. But Natasha was a Leading Bird Citizen of the city, so she lived and worked on top of the landmark.

Nowadays people come to India by aeroplane, but long ago they came in ships and landed at the Gateway of India. You can see in history books that Natasha's great-uncle Raghu (1,397 bird generations back) was the first pigeon of the British Raj to do potty on the Prince of Wales when he visited India in 1908.

Natasha's work made her travel. Sometimes she had to carry coffee samples to South America, sometimes she took tea bags to China, sometimes she flew lamb kababs to New Zealand. She was the fastest courier pigeon in the whole world. She always delivered packets right on time, no matter how far she had to fly, even when the weather was so bad that the big aeroplanes didn't take off. All the birds of India were proud of Natasha.

Pigeons are wonderful navigators, like the drivers of school buses. They can read maps and find the way to any place. Long back, there were carrier pigeons who carried messages written on paper and tied to their legs.

They were Air Mail in the days before there were any aeroplanes. But each carrier pigeon is good only for one route.

Natasha was not like that – she was a Courier Pigeon. Couriers have to take letters and packets to all parts of the country and all over the world. They need to know how to reach any place they are asked to go to. They have to know all the air routes, and that is much, much harder than ordinary pigeon navigation.

Nani Kevinino, a green Naga pigeon, had been the first qualified pilot in India's North-East. She was the first to fly from Guwahati to Dhaka and from Kathmandu to Kohima. She was the one who opened up the air routes which other birds followed later, and then aeroplanes.

After she retired from service, Nani Kevinino started a Flying School in the roof of Victoria Terminus, which was Mumbai's biggest railway station. She was very famous, so lots and lots of birds came to her school to study. Birds came from other countries too. Once there was a whole class full of Siberian Cranes. Another time, two Emus turned up; but they never learnt to fly properly.

Nani's Flying School was not only for birds. Bees came there to learn, and also yellow and red and blue butterflies.

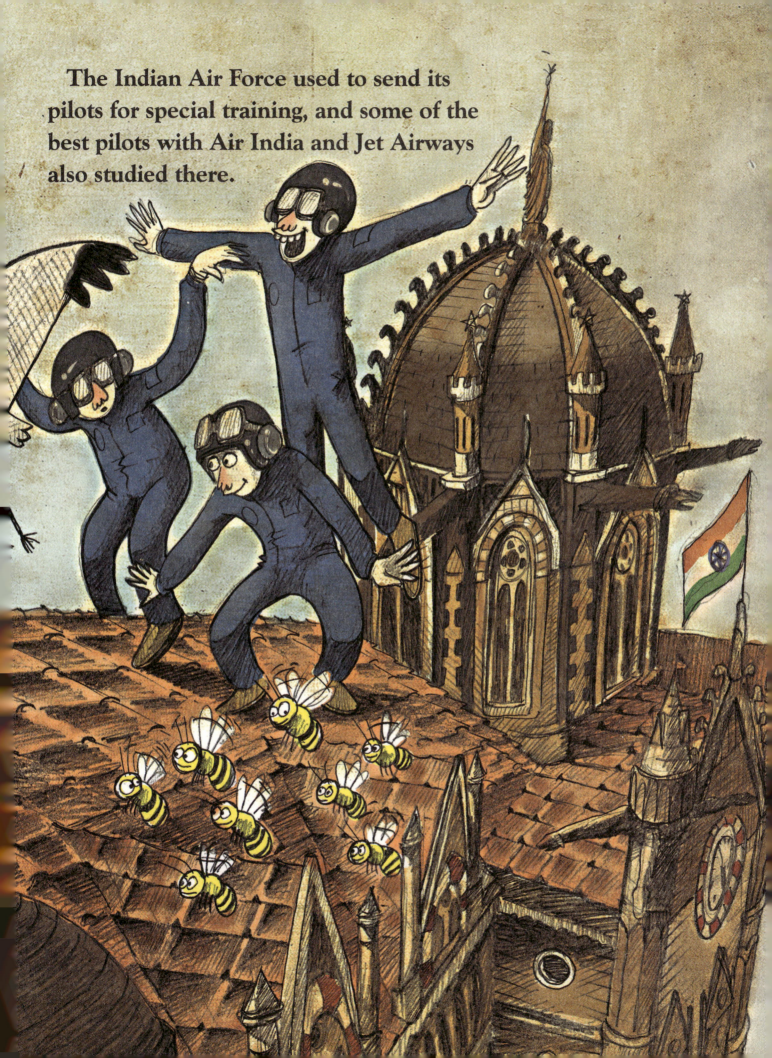

The Indian Air Force used to send its pilots for special training, and some of the best pilots with Air India and Jet Airways also studied there.

At the school, Natasha learnt everything very quickly, and she never forgot anything. She was a brilliant pupil, maybe even the best the school ever had. She was selected to lead the Indian Bird Circus, an aerobatic team which flew at the Independence Day and Republic Day parades. In Delhi, she led the whole Air Force team. The aeroplanes flew over India Gate and the birds flew through it.

Natasha knew every air route by heart, and she was very good at drawing maps too. She would hold pencils and rubbers with her feet and an ink pen in her beak, and she would hop and skip over the paper, and soon a clean and neat map would be ready.

All flyers need maps, and Natasha's maps were the best. The towns and rivers and mountains were marked, and all the good trees on which tired birds could rest for a while. On every route Natasha would mark with a big red X every house of nice people who put out water and seeds in their gardens for the birds who flew that way.

So, you see, Natasha was very busy, because she ran both a courier service and a map-making office. She had seventeen courier birds, of whom the best was an old puffin from Middlesex, and five cartographers, of whom the best was Mike Mercator, a parrot from the Amazon forest who drew only circles.

That's enough for now. Next time I'll tell you about how Natasha and Sher Singh travelled right across the ocean, under the water, all the way to South Africa, and how they drew a fine map for submariners to follow.

And oh yes, about Razia and her ... I'll tell you that one next time.

Crossword Time!

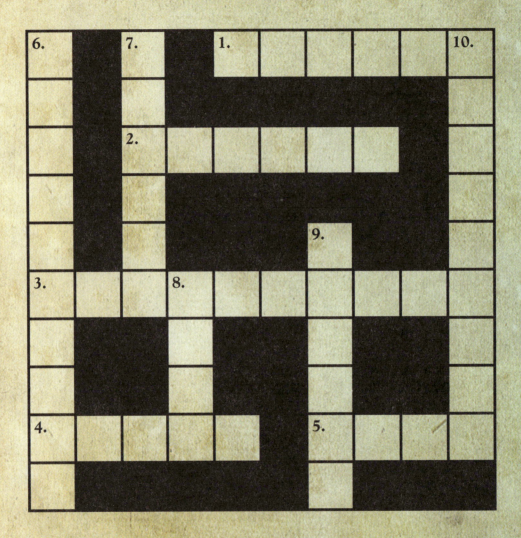

Across

01. The Land of coconut trees (6)
02. Origin of Lamb's and other Kabab recipes took place here (6)
03. Holtville, _____ is called the carrot capital of the world (10)
04. Tea originated here (5)
05. Son music, precursor of Salsa, originated here (4)

Down

06. The homeland of Penguins (10)
07. The largest producer of Coffee (6)
08. Formerly called Persia, the pioneers of using the Pigeon Communication Network (4)
09. The word Cartography (chartis = map; graphein = write) was coined here (6)
10. Where boomerang was invented (9)

ANSWERS ON NEXT PAGE

Find all the places the story takes you to!

Mukul Dube has a big grey beard. His friends, mostly little girls, pretend to visit him but spend their time playing with his puppy Goofy, who is also a little girl. When he was young he played nearly every game there was – except cricket, because he never did understand how many balls there were in an over. He has been using cameras since he was 10, and for some years he was a professional photographer. He has been a teacher too, and as an editor he has messed up the writing of many people. He has the tools he needs for the small electrical, mechanical and carpentry jobs he does now and then. He likes to cook, and he also likes to think that people like his cooking. Anyone can see that he writes rubbish.

Fahad Faizal shares his Mumbai home with his good friend and companion, a white cat Elizabeth. They work together, play together, and even eat fish together! Fahad was born in Kerala and graduated from the National Institute of Design at Ahmedabad, with a degree in Animation Film Design. He has interned with Walt Disney India and worked for Miditech Delhi on animation design projects. He currently works as a freelance animation designer.

KATHA

First published in 2011
Copyright © Katha, 2011
Text copyright © Mukul Dube, 2011
Illustrations copyright © Fahad Faizal, 2011
All rights reserved. No part of this book may be reproduced or utilized in any form without the prior written permission of the publisher.
Printed at RaveIndia, New Delhi
ISBN 978-81-89934-77-4

KATHA is a registered nonprofit devoted to enhancing the joys of reading amongst children and adults. Katha Schools are situated in the slums and streets of Delhi and tribal villages of Arunachal Pradesh.
A3 Sarvodaya Enclave, Sri Aurobindo Marg
New Delhi 110 017
Phone: 4141 6600 . 4182 9998 . 2652 1752
Fax: 2651 4373
E-mail: marketing@katha.org, Website: www.katha.org

This book is supported by the Department of School Education & Literacy, Ministry of Human Resource Development, Government of India.
Ten per cent of sales proceeds from this book will support the quality education of children studying in Katha Schools.
Katha regularly plants trees to replace the wood used in the making of its books.

First Reprint 2014

ANSWERS
Across: 1. KERALA 2. ARABIA 3. CALIFORNIA 4. CHINA 5. CUBA
Down: 6. ANTARCTICA 7. BRAZIL 8. IRAN 9. GREECE 10. AUSTRALIA

More exciting elephant stories ... straight from Katha's treasure chest!

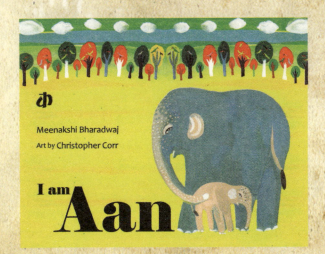

I am Aan
Meenakshi Bharadwaj

Deep in the jungles of the Western Ghats lives a baby elephant called Aan. Here's a heart-warming story of Aan as he embarks on his journey from the magical world of childhood to the tough adult one.

Punctuated with facts on elephants, Aan's exciting voyage of self-discovery will sure make him great friends with young readers.

Full of interesting facts and trivia on elephants this is a book that nature loving kids will treasure. The illustrations by Christopher Corr are bright and vivid. Flatteringly, he says he discovered colour in India.
— Saffron Tree

Aan, a male elephant, tells his story in first person, starting at his birth and introducing you to his family. It talks of his childish boisterousness and how he was forced to grow up, focusing on how growing up isn't always easy or fun. Packed with elephant facts and trivia, it is a good read for young nature-lovers. — Time Out

The Elephant in the Tree
Mallika Nagarajan

With its quirky characters, unusual use of language and skilful blending of fantasy and reality, this is a lovely story of Mahi who finds a seven-trunked elephant in the tree and journeys with him into a new world that will change her life forever. Mallika's delightfully illustrated story shows us how each one of us, like Mahi, is also capable of great little miracles. So come, be a miracle worker. And see how well you can do it!

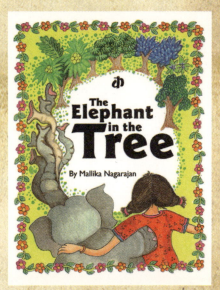

Katha books always offer beautiful illustrations with riots of colours which are sure way to have dedicated young readers spending hours and hours savouring the details of each picture.
— Literary Sojourn

The simple text and expressive pictures with a lot of details will make the child want to look at the book over and over again, each time noticing something new and exciting – a monkey on a tree, a snake coiled on the branch of a tree, tiny butterflies and more. What a delightful way to deliver this strong message of conservation to kids!
— Young India Book